Introduction

Chapter 1: Take Charge of the Buying Process

Chapter 2: It All Begins with the Squeeze Page

Chapter 3: Offer a Directly-Related Paid Product Deal

Chapter 4: Time to Introduce an Upsell or Downsell Offer

Chapter 5: Set Up Your Autoresponder Follow-Up Sequence

Chapter 6: Testing Your Sales Funnel to Ensure It Works Perfectly

Chapter 7: Launching Your New Product

Conclusion

Introduction

You've likely heard that owning your own product is key to making real money online.

This is true for several reasons, but primarily because when you own the product, you have full control over the sales funnel. This control allows you to profit directly, often at 100%, or in conjunction with any affiliate commissions you may choose to offer. In contrast, if you're selling someone else's product, you don't control the funnel or earn from any additional sales made through it.

It's a well-known fact that most Internet marketers

make the majority of their profits not on the front end, but on the back end of the sales funnel. In some cases, marketers are even willing to take a loss on the initial sale just to acquire new customers and motivate affiliates to promote future offers. This approach works because the real profits come from upsells, which are higher-priced offers presented after the initial sale.

The back end of the funnel often includes one-time offers (OTOs), where marketers make 50-100% of the sale. This is why the bulk of a marketer's revenue is generated after the first purchase. If you're serious about making significant money online, owning your product and controlling the sales funnel is essential.

Relying solely on affiliate marketing limits your earning potential, as your profits are capped by the decisions of the product owner and the structure of their sales funnel. By owning your funnel, you have the power to create a system that maximizes your profits and rewards affiliates who help promote your offers.

If you're wondering how to build and optimize your own sales funnel, this book will guide you step by step. You'll learn what a sales funnel is, how to create one, and most importantly, how to maximize its potential to generate the highest possible profit.

Chapter 1: Take Charge of the Buying Process

As highlighted in the Introduction, if you don't take control of the sales funnel, you risk being left behind by those who are already profiting online. Many experienced internet marketers emphasize the importance of selling your own digital products. By doing so, you essentially control the entire sales funnel, which is key to generating consistent income online.

To gain this control, you must first create your own digital product and then establish a sales funnel around it. The sales funnel is more than just a straightforward product sale—it's a system designed to offer multiple products or services to your customer at various stages of the buying process. This means that in addition to your main product offer, you'll typically include one or more additional offers, often referred to as upsells or one-time offers (OTOs).

An upsell is an upgraded or more advanced version of your original product. It gives your customer the option to enhance their experience or gain additional value. While traditionally, sales funnels included only one upsell or OTO, modern funnels often feature several additional offers, sometimes as many as three to ten. These can include both upsells and downsells. A downsell is a more affordable version of the upsell, offering some of the additional features but at a lower price point.

There are two essential rules for creating successful sales funnels. First, your upsells and downsells should be directly related to the main product. This ensures that each offer adds extra value to the customer's original purchase. Second, these offers should be optional. The customer should still receive the full value of the main product without feeling obligated to buy the upsell or downsell.

When you create a well-structured sales funnel, you increase your chances of generating more revenue with each customer interaction. Not everyone will buy your upsells, but research shows that many customers are more likely to make additional purchases right after buying the main product. This is similar to how people often buy fries or a drink along with a hamburger, or choose a higher-end version of a product to get more value out of it.

The key to success lies in getting as many people as possible to purchase your main offer. Once a customer has committed to that first purchase, they are more likely to consider buying one or more upsells, especially if you present them with attractive downsell options. Studies also show that offering a lower-priced version of an upsell can appeal to customers who are looking for value, making them more likely to purchase.

Taking control of your sales funnel is essential to building a profitable online business. The more effectively you can manage the buying process, the faster you can grow your income. In addition, a well-optimized sales funnel not only leads to more sales but also helps you grow a loyal customer base, allowing you to continue selling to them in the future.

Chapter 2: It All Begins with the Squeeze Page

The foundation of any effective sales funnel starts with the squeeze page. A squeeze page is a simple web page designed to offer something valuable to visitors in exchange for their contact information, typically their name and email address. This page serves as a gateway to begin building a relationship with potential customers by delivering something they perceive as beneficial, like a free report or guide on a topic of interest.

The key purpose of a squeeze page is to entice visitors to voluntarily share their contact details. By doing so, you gain the ability to follow up with them, sending relevant and useful information that helps you establish trust and demonstrate your expertise in your niche or industry. Over time, as subscribers become more familiar with you and confident in your knowledge, they are more likely to consider purchasing the offers you present. These offers can include your own products as well as affiliate products you recommend.

While affiliate offers can generate income, the real profits come from promoting your own digital products. Your goal is to nurture your relationship with subscribers so that they feel comfortable buying from you. If you approach this carefully, without overwhelming or misleading your audience, you can build a loyal customer base that will return to you for future offers, thus creating a long-term source of income.

In order to convince visitors to provide their contact information on the squeeze page, you need to offer something valuable for free. This could be a mini-report, a guide, or even an eBook that addresses a problem or need relevant to your audience.

You can create this free product yourself, hire someone to do it, or use private label rights (PLR) content that you can customize for your offer. The key point is that the content must be valuable enough to entice people to give up their contact information willingly.

Your squeeze page should clearly outline what the visitor will receive when they submit their information. For example, if you're offering a report on how to drive more qualified traffic to a website, make sure the page highlights this specific benefit. Once they submit their information, an automated system (known as an autoresponder) will send them the promised content. Depending on your setup, you might use a single opt-in system, where the content is delivered immediately, or a double opt-in system, where the user must confirm their email address before receiving the content.

The effectiveness of the squeeze page hinges on how valuable the free offer appears to the visitor. If they see genuine value in the free product, they'll be more inclined to share their contact information. However, if it doesn't resonate with them, they likely won't. That's why the free gift must be directly aligned with the interests and needs of your audience.

It's important to note that while the free product should be valuable, it shouldn't give away everything about the topic. If the free offer provides all the answers, subscribers won't have a reason to buy any of your paid products. Instead, the free report should give them a taste of the solution they're seeking while hinting that you have more in-depth information available for purchase. At the end of the report, you can include a link to your main product's sales page, encouraging them to explore further and potentially make a purchase.

In summary, the squeeze page is the critical first step in your sales funnel. It allows you to gather contact information, build trust, and guide potential customers toward your paid products. The more effectively you craft your squeeze page and free offer, the more successful you'll be in converting visitors into loyal customers.

Chapter 3: Offer a Directly-Related Paid Product Deal

After your subscriber submits their contact information on the squeeze page, they should be directed to a page confirming that the free report they signed up for is on its way to their inbox. This marks the beginning of your relationship with the subscriber. To build this relationship, you must employ effective email marketing techniques, fostering trust and demonstrating your expertise in your industry.

Research shows that it often takes at least seven touchpoints with a prospect before they are willing to make a purchase. This means you can't expect someone to buy a product after one or two interactions; instead, you need to engage them over time with valuable content. While some people may be ready to purchase after just a few interactions, others may need more than seven. There will also be those who never buy at all. It all depends on the individual's mindset, circumstances, and level of interest.

The key to generating sales lies in building a relationship with your subscriber through thoughtful and consistent follow-up. Expecting them to become a loyal customer overnight is unrealistic. Therefore, after they've downloaded your free report, you should continue to deliver valuable information through follow-up emails. These emails should ensure that they received the report, provide additional insights into the problem or issue they're facing, and subtly hint that the solution lies in the paid product you offer.

It's also essential to let subscribers know that you're available to answer any questions they might have. This creates an open line of communication, reinforcing the idea that you are a trusted expert in your field. Offering advice and assistance for free further strengthens this perception, making it more likely that they'll view your paid product as a valuable resource worth purchasing.

As you continue nurturing the relationship, some of your subscribers will eventually be ready to buy. This is why it's important to include a link to your main product offer in every email. However, it's crucial not to "hard-sell" your product in every message. Aggressive marketing can turn off your subscribers and may even cause them to unsubscribe. Instead, reserve hard-selling for one or two emails in a series of seven, and use the remaining emails to offer helpful information and advice.

Your follow-up emails should focus on providing value, addressing the prospect's problems, and offering steps they can take to address their issues. The link to your product should be included at the end of these emails, but in a subtle way. Most people are put off by overly aggressive marketing tactics, so if you repeatedly push your product too hard, you risk losing the prospect altogether.

If a subscriber chooses to unsubscribe, you've lost a potential customer forever. That's why the focus should always be on educating and helping the prospect rather than pressuring them into making a purchase. By doing so, you increase the likelihood that, over time, they will see the value in your product and make the decision to buy on their own terms.

Once the prospect recognizes the worth of your product, they will click the link in one of your emails and make a purchase. At this point, the prospect transforms into a paying customer, and they've officially entered your sales funnel. Now, the real potential of your sales funnel begins to unfold as you have the opportunity to continue selling additional products and offers to this customer, maximizing the value of your relationship with them.

Chapter 4: Time to Introduce an Upsell or Downsell Offer

Once a prospect transitions into a customer by purchasing your main product, they've officially entered your sales funnel. This is the perfect moment to present an opportunity for them to "upgrade" their order through a value-enhancing upsell that complements the main product they just bought. An upsell could be an enhanced version of the original offer, like a more comprehensive ebook, additional features in a software program, or a more in-depth video course. The idea is to provide more value to what the customer has already purchased.

Another effective strategy is to offer a related product as the upsell. For example, if your main product is a traffic generation course, an upsell could be an email marketing course designed to help convert that traffic into sales. The upsell is not an essential purchase, but it should be presented as a logical next step, something that enhances the effectiveness of the original product. It's important that the main product delivers the value it promised without requiring any additional purchases. Making upsells mandatory to achieve the value of the original product is unethical and can tarnish your reputation. Therefore, all upsells and downsells must remain optional.

When done correctly, upsells offer additional value at a price that customers find enticing, which increases the likelihood of a purchase. If the upsell is successful, the customer will be directed to a page where they can access both the main product and the upsell. Alternatively, they could be offered another upsell related to the main product. If they decline the upsell, several pathways are available. You can either direct them to the download page for the main product, present them with another upsell, or offer them a downsell—a modified version of the upsell at a lower price.

A downsell usually differs from the upsell in some way, often offering fewer features or content, but at a more attractive price. In some cases, the downsell may be identical to the upsell but priced lower. This is less common, but effective when the customer shows interest in the upsell but hesitates due to the price. Research shows that consumers don't like to miss out on offers entirely. By providing a second chance to purchase a similar product at a lower price, you increase the likelihood of converting a hesitant customer.

This is why many internet marketers include corresponding downsells with their upsells—it boosts the chances of conversions and maximizes the potential revenue from each customer. Having a mix of upsells and downsells throughout your sales funnel is an effective way to increase profits. Some customers may decline every upsell or downsell, while others may purchase one or several of each.

The inclusion of both upsells and downsells in your sales funnel increases your opportunities for conversions, leading to more revenue. As many seasoned marketers know, the bulk of their profits often come from the back-end of the funnel—

through upsells and downsells—rather than from the front-end, which consists of the main product. These additional offers ensure that you're maximizing the lifetime value of each customer who enters your funnel, turning a one-time purchase into multiple revenue opportunities.

Chapter 5: Set Up Your Autoresponder Follow-Up Sequence

Once your prospect has downloaded the free report from your squeeze page, it's crucial to follow up with them to build a relationship and nurture trust. This process is done through a sequence of follow-up emails, typically consisting of seven messages. The first message should be sent immediately after the prospect provides their contact information (or after confirming it if using a double opt-in system).

To automate this process and make it more efficient, set up your emails in an autoresponder. This way, each email is sent at scheduled intervals without you needing to manually send them. The first email in this sequence should thank the subscriber for requesting the free report and include a link to download it. In this email, you should also mention that you'll follow up with more useful information and relevant offers related to their problem or industry, and provide your contact details in case they have questions.

In the following emails, focus on providing valuable information regarding the issue or topic discussed in the free report. Each email should offer insights or suggestions for addressing the problem. You should also subtly include a link to your main product offer's sales page as a solution for solving the issue in a more comprehensive manner. However, avoid pushing too hard on sales in every email.

Out of the seven follow-up emails, only two should be "hard-sell" emails, typically the fourth and seventh in the sequence. These hard-sell emails should focus on explaining how your main product can provide a complete solution to the issue the prospect is facing. For example, if the issue is about generating quality traffic for a website, you might emphasize that your product includes proven methods to drive high-quality traffic that will make the prospect's traffic woes disappear.

However, hard-selling in every email can be counterproductive. Aggressively promoting your product too often may push your prospects away, potentially causing them to unsubscribe from your list. Once they unsubscribe, the relationship ends, and you lose the chance to convert them into a paying customer.

To avoid this, always prioritize value over aggressive sales tactics. When prospects see that the free information you're providing is valuable, they are more likely to assume that your paid products are even more valuable. This thought process leads them to trust your recommendations, making it easier to eventually convince them to purchase your main product offer.

The ultimate goal of your follow-up sequence is to make your subscribers comfortable with your expertise and trust your guidance. As they grow more familiar with you and see the value in your information, they'll be more inclined to buy your products, enter your sales funnel, and potentially purchase upsells and downsells. This is how top internet marketers generate most of their income, allowing them to enjoy the freedom of the "Internet lifestyle" without the constraints of a traditional 9-5 job.

By mastering the art of follow-up emails, you'll not only establish a solid relationship with your prospects but also create an effective system that consistently converts leads into paying customers.

Chapter 6: Testing Your Sales Funnel to Ensure It Works Perfectly

One common mistake many new internet marketers make is failing to thoroughly test their sales funnel before launching it. Too often, marketers only realize something is wrong when a customer or subscriber informs them that the funnel is broken. By the time they discover these issues, they may have already lost significant revenue opportunities.

A broken sales funnel means potential customers might encounter obstacles during their purchase journey, such as not receiving the correct follow-up emails or being improperly routed through upsells and downsells. Unfortunately, once customers leave a funnel, especially after experiencing problems, the chances of getting them back are slim. This is particularly true if the funnel includes time-sensitive offers or one-time upsell and downsell opportunities, which are typically presented only after a customer purchases the main product. Once a customer exits the funnel, those profit-boosting opportunities vanish.

Moreover, failing to test your sales funnel can harm your reputation as an internet marketer. Word can quickly spread that your funnels are unreliable, which can damage your credibility. This can affect your ability to secure joint ventures, attract new customers, and retain subscribers. In the competitive world of online marketing, building a reputation for professionalism and reliability is crucial for long-term success.

Given these risks, thoroughly testing your funnel before launching your product or offer is a step you can't afford to skip. Testing helps ensure that all components of the funnel—from initial lead capture to post-purchase upsell offers—work flawlessly.

How to Test Your Funnel

Start by going through the ordering process as if you were a customer. If your funnel includes a free offer on your squeeze page (such as a free report), request it. Ensure you receive the promised report, either as a direct download or via email, and verify that your follow-up email sequence is triggered correctly.

Next, purchase the main product yourself to confirm that you receive the appropriate follow-up email with the download link or access instructions. This is also where you should check if you're correctly routed to the first upsell offer. Most sales platforms, such as ClickBank, JVZoo, and WarriorPlus, offer testing options that allow you to pay a minimal amount (like $0 or $0.01) to simulate a real purchase and test the funnel.

Beyond the main product, test all upsell and downsell offers in the funnel. Make sure that when you purchase an upsell, the next offer in the sequence is displayed. Likewise, decline each offer to confirm that customers who reject the upsell or downsell are correctly routed to the appropriate next step. This ensures that all customers, regardless of their purchase decisions, are presented with the correct offers in the funnel. The goal is to maximize profit potential by ensuring a smooth and seamless journey through the sales process for every customer.

Don't Test Alone

It's a good idea to ask other experienced marketers to test your funnel as well. While your own testing is essential, getting a fresh set of eyes on the process can reveal issues you might have overlooked. They may spot glitches or inefficiencies in your funnel that could hinder customer satisfaction or reduce profits.

Remember, if your sales funnel breaks down at any point during the customer's journey, you not only lose that sale but also the potential for additional profits from upsells, downsells, and follow-up offers. Recovering from these lost opportunities is nearly impossible. Therefore, it's worth double- and even triple-checking that every aspect of your sales funnel works as intended.

Check Your Emails

Don't forget to test the email sequence as well. Every time a customer makes a purchase—whether it's the main product or an upsell—there should be a follow-up email sent with the product download link or other necessary information. If these emails fail to arrive, customers are likely to become frustrated, which could damage your relationship with them and harm your brand. Ensure these emails are being delivered properly and promptly, so your customers feel confident in their purchase and receive everything they were promised.

In conclusion, testing your sales funnel is an essential step in ensuring that it functions flawlessly. By testing every aspect of the process, from the initial opt-in to the final upsell offer, you can avoid potential pitfalls, maximize your profits, and build a strong, trustworthy reputation in the online marketing world.

Chapter 7: Launching Your New Product

Once you've confirmed that your sales funnel is working smoothly, with all relevant emails being sent correctly for each purchase, it's time for the exciting next step: launching your new product! This is when you can finally set the prices of each offer throughout your funnel to their intended amounts, moving away from the $0 or $0.01 test price.

With everything set, the focus shifts to promotion. You need to spread the word and get your product in front of as many potential customers as possible. Here are the key methods you can use to promote your launch:

- **Email Marketing**: Your email list is one of your most powerful tools. Send out a well-crafted email campaign, introducing your product, highlighting its benefits, and including strong calls-to-action to encourage purchases.

- **Social Media**: Platforms like Facebook, Instagram, Twitter, and LinkedIn are essential for promoting your product. Leverage these networks to share content about your product, engage with your audience, and encourage shares to expand your reach.

- **Forum Marketing**: Participate in online communities or forums relevant to your niche. Provide value in discussions while subtly promoting your product when appropriate.

- **Blog/Newsletter**: If you maintain a blog or regularly send newsletters, now's the time to feature your new product. Create content that highlights how your product solves your audience's problems.

- **Paid Advertising**: Consider using paid ads on platforms like Google Ads or social media channels to drive targeted traffic to your sales funnel. Ads can be a quick way to get attention if you target the right audience.

- **Joint Ventures**: Partnering with other marketers or businesses who share a similar audience can significantly increase your reach. Offer them an affiliate commission for promoting your product to their list or network.

The key here is to let the world know that your product offers a solution to the problems your target audience is facing. Position your product as the answer to their challenges, helping them reduce stress and improve their lives. Make it clear that it's available and ready to be purchased immediately.

Using Testimonials to Boost Credibility

If you've had beta-testers or early users of your product, be sure to include their feedback in your marketing materials. Testimonials are a powerful tool for overcoming buyer skepticism. They demonstrate that real people have already tried your product and found it effective. This can significantly reduce hesitation and build trust with your potential customers.

People are often uncertain whether a product will work as promised, or whether they can trust the seller. Testimonials can help alleviate these doubts, showing that your product is the real deal. Be sure to highlight any positive reviews from beta-testers or users of previous versions of your product to reinforce the idea that your product delivers on its promises.

Monitor and Optimize Your Funnel

Even after your product is launched, the work is far from over. Now, it's time to closely monitor how your offers are performing throughout your sales funnel. This is where analytics tools come into play. Platforms like Google Analytics, which is free, allow you to track conversions and identify any bottlenecks in your funnel.

Understanding which parts of your funnel are converting well—and which aren't—is crucial. If certain offers (whether it's the main product, an upsell, or a downsell) are underperforming, it's important to figure out why. Is it the offer itself? The pricing? The sales copy? Maybe the product isn't resonating with your target audience the way you thought it would. Pinpointing these issues will allow you to make adjustments and improve your funnel's overall performance.

Continuous Improvement for Long-Term Success

Launching your product is just the beginning. Once your funnel is live, you need to gather data on what's working and what's not. Analyze conversion rates, customer behavior, and feedback to identify areas for improvement. By doing this, you can optimize your funnel, boosting its profitability over time.

Moreover, the insights you gain from this process will help you refine future sales funnels. The more you learn from each launch, the better positioned you'll be to design even more effective funnels that drive higher conversions and greater profits right from the start.

In summary, a successful product launch requires careful planning, consistent promotion, and ongoing analysis. By promoting your product effectively, leveraging testimonials, and constantly optimizing your funnel, you'll maximize your chances of success and set the stage for even greater profitability in future launches.

Conclusion

In this e-book, we have explored the vital importance of controlling your sales funnel and how having your own product can lead to significantly higher profits in the online marketplace. By taking control of your funnel, you can shape the customer journey from start to finish, ensuring that every step maximizes your profit potential.

We began by discussing how the sales funnel process starts with a simple yet powerful tool: the squeeze page. This page captures the interest of prospects by offering a free report on an industry issue or problem that resonates with them. From here, you initiate the follow-up process through email marketing, using an autoresponder to establish your authority in the field and build trust with your audience.

A key takeaway is the principle that it takes, on average, seven points of contact to convert a prospect into a paying customer. However, it's essential not to overwhelm potential buyers with constant hard-sell messages. Consumers today prefer value-driven interactions. Thus, a well-balanced email marketing strategy includes no more than two hard-sell emails out of every seven. The majority of your communication should focus on providing helpful, quality content that positions you as a reliable expert. Including a subtle link to your main product's sales page with a brief mention of its benefits at the end of each email can encourage prospects to explore your offer without feeling pressured.

Over time, if you consistently provide valuable information, some of your prospects will be inclined to make a purchase. They may reason, "If the free content is this good, the paid product must be even better." This moment represents the tipping point in your funnel: once they purchase the main product, they are immediately presented with additional opportunities for upsells.

The upsell process allows you to offer complementary products that enhance the value of the main offer. If the customer sees value in the upsell and makes another purchase, they may be presented with additional upsells. This process continues until they reach the end of your funnel. For each purchase, the customer will receive the appropriate follow-up emails, including links to download their products.

If a customer declines an upsell, you can strategically offer a downsell—a similar product or the same product at a reduced price. Many customers find downsells appealing because they feel like they're getting a better deal, and this can lead to additional sales that might not have happened otherwise. However, keep in mind that not every customer will purchase upsells or downsells, and that's perfectly fine. Your goal is to maximize the profit potential of each customer who enters your funnel, regardless of their individual choices.

One of the most critical steps before launching your product is ensuring that your sales funnel works flawlessly. There's no way to recover a lost sale if a customer encounters a broken funnel, whether it's for the main product or any of the upsells and downsells. Thoroughly test your funnel yourself and enlist other experienced marketers to test it as well to ensure that everything functions as intended. This will guarantee that customers are presented with every offer in your funnel, maximizing your chances of making additional sales.

Once you're confident that your funnel is ready, it's time to launch your product. Promote it through a variety of channels, including email marketing, social media, paid advertising, forum participation, joint ventures, and more. The key is to get your product in front of as many eyes as possible.

After the launch, the work continues. Carefully monitor how each part of your funnel performs. Identify which offers are converting well and which are underperforming. By analyzing this data, you can make informed adjustments to improve your current funnel's profitability and learn valuable lessons for future product launches.

By following the steps outlined in this ebook, you now have the knowledge to create and control a sales funnel that maximizes the profit potential of each customer. With careful planning, testing, and optimization, you can build highly profitable product offers and ensure long-term success.

Good luck, and may your sales funnels lead to greater success and profitability!

www.ingramcontent.com/pod-product-compliance
Lightning Source LLC
Chambersburg PA
CBHW070955220526
45471CB00007B/3036